ABIDE

a 21-day study on friendship

andrea lebeau

Praise for Abide

Beautiful, charming and engaging, Andrea gets right to the heart of friendship. We were created to be in relationship and community with God and each other. This simple yet deep study helps us identify the issues that hold us back from experiencing both. Her learn-from-my-mistakes vulnerability is refreshing and her light hearted approach keeps it real and honest. "Abide" will challenge, encourage and equip you to cultivate and strengthen your friendships all while causing you to feel like you're having coffee with Andrea at her kitchen table.

Amy Wiggins, Pastor, Rez.Church

When I was young, I understood the importance of friendship, but it wasn't until becoming an adult that I grasped the deep gift that doing life with other like-hearted women truly is. Andrea also comprehends this. Leaning heavily on God through scripture, she encourages us to grow roots as we strive to live stronger and more generous friendships that for decades to come.

Teresa Swanstrom Anderson,
author of Beautifully Interuppted

Andrea has a way with her heart and words that draw you and make you feel like she is speaking truth over your life. She is vulnerable and raw in a way that is desperately needed in this generation. The words on these pages peel back her own journey layer by layer, they are situations most all of us have been in and needed guidance to get through. She is the girl next door that you want to raise your babies with and and walk through life figuring it all out together. She is fun, honest, and a true sister in Christ. Go grab your coffee and cozy up, because Andrea assures us that we are welcome and wanted here.

Casey Zaruba, author and inspirational speaker

When I read through this study, Abide, I found myself both challenged & encouraged. Challenged to be a more intentional friend; one who invests and takes time to really develop life giving relationships. And encouraged through the many Bible verses and prayers that fill the pages of the study. I love how real Andrea is and that she writes in a way that is relatable, genuine and fun! There is no doubt that Abide came from God's heart and that it will bring encouragement & healing to everyone who reads it!

Kaitlyn Scott, Women's Pastor at

I have never met someone who is more real than Andrea. She has a way with words that will inspire you and bring you to tears at the same time. After reading Abide, I felt like I had learned so much about myself that I had never realized. I feel more empowered than ever to be a better friend. Abide makes me feel like I'm sitting across from my amazing friend, Andrea, having a good cup of coffee. I am so excited for women around the world to read this amazing devotional. I know without a doubt that it will change your friendships forever. I love the truth that is spoken about our amazing Creator, and I'm so thankful for Andrea's beautiful way of putting it all to words. I know exactly the devotional that I will be passing on to all my friends!

Christie Rose, founder of @shepaintstruth_

Editor:
Rachel Gonzalez

Cover photo:
Andrea LeBeau

Special thanks to:
Rhema Peterson & Brittany Scheer

ISBN-13: 978-1983777301
ISBN-10: 1983777307

CONTENTS

Day 1 | Redeemed 6

Day 2 | Companionship 11

Day 3 | Create 14

Day 4 | Confidence 17

Day 5 | Support 21

Day 6 | Cultivate 25

Day 7 | Adult Friends 28

Day 8 | Seasons 32

Day 9 | Bad Apples 36

Day 10 | Forgiveness 39

Day 11 | I Got You, Babe 42

Day 12 | Gossip 45

Day 13 | Therapy 48

Day 14 | Gather 51

Day 15 | Pray 54

Day 16 | Serve Your Friends 58

Day 17 | Communion 62

Day 18 | Love Your Friends 66

Day 19 | Comparison 70

Day 20 | Treat Yo' Self 74

Day 21 | Abide 78

──DAY ONE──

Redeemed

I am a former mean girl. I didn't realize it at the time - I was trying to fit in, I was being funny, I was acting cool.

At times, I have been the best friend you could ask for. Are you sick? Care package on your doorstep with chicken noodle soup, magazines, and a cozy blanket. Miscarriage? I can't get the flowers to you fast enough. I'm a gift-giver, and when there is a need, I want to step in.

On the flipside, I have been the worst kind of friend you could imagine. Talking behind your back? Judgmental? Jealous? D - all of the above.

It took great loss of friendships for God to redeem what I didn't know was broken.

I moved to Colorado when I was 22 years old. I knew only the family who came with me, and the people I worked with.

I quickly became involved in church, but it wasn't until a few years had passed that I made a good girlfriend. I cried and prayed and cried and prayed for a friend who was like me, for someone who would go to Target with me just for the heck of it, and for someone who would be constant in my life.

My prayer was answered, and it was really good, but life got in the way. Choices and life began to shift the temperature of my relationship, and with a big heave ho on my part, the friendship fizzled after five years of friendship. We shared everything - miscarriages, marital problems, family issues, job promotions, births, deaths, and everything in between. One day, it all changed, and I was alone.

You may think that's bad enough, but I also used this time to mean girl. I was hurt, lost, and angry, and I took it out on people that I loved. In one month, I went from being loved to shunned. If I look back on that season, I think of it as a light bulb turning off in a small room. I was utterly alone, and it was completely my fault.

After a few months had passed, the sadness was eating away at me. We had just moved to a new house, and the stress that had taken on our family was palpable. I had dreams of filling our new home with friends, and there was no one. It was quiet, empty, and lonely. I was desperate. I hadn't been to church consistently in a while, and I knew I needed to at least find a Bible study to get a little human interaction. I called my girlfriend, Rhema, who had been leading a table at a local church, and asked if she had space for me at her table.

I pleaded with her that I needed "friennnnds! Normal people who have kids, preferably." She just happened to have a space for me, and so I went. I had a known some of the gals for a few years, and so it was easy to slip back into conversation. It was easy and enjoyable, but I knew they weren't the ones who'd shoulder burdens or be there for the long haul.

I stayed consistent, and found myself excited to go to Bible study each week. I even ended up back at church, and loved it. I enjoyed my time, our monthly outings, and some girls' night here and there, but I was still slowly retreating. I shared what I wanted to share - what was safe, and really enjoyed the laughter and interaction. What they didn't know was that when I would get in my car to leave, I'd pray someone would hit me. I was lost, hurt, broken, and tangibly empty. I wasn't going to hurt myself, but I prayed the agony would end for me.

It wasn't until October of this year that God radically and totally changed my heart. You see, I grew up believing in the Old Testament God - fire and brimstone, pillar of salt kind of stuff. I knew many people, my husband included, who had this sweet, intimate relationship with a kind and loving God, but I had yet to have an experience like theirs. It was probably too late for me, and so I carried on. Sitting in an auditorium at a business conference, the Lord met me in the most tangible, precious way. He showed me my heart being cleaned out - the lies, the hurts, the anguish I had felt. He gave me vision after vision of His hand on my back, guiding me to different places over the past year. The loss of my friendships was actually the first step. I had seen it as Him taking things away from me - a punishment for being "bad." When in reality, when the puzzle finally came together, He had ordained each step as He gently guided me to redemption.

And in that Hilton hotel, God gave me the clearest vision for the calling on my life: women's ministry - to empower them, give them a platform, and give them a voice outside of marriage and motherhood. I have had a pull towards women for years, but I was never able to put it into practice. God knew that I needed to hit some low lows to be able to minister to women effectively.

I will tell you that it has been met multiple times with attitude. "You were mean. Good luck 'empowering women.'" In those moments, I want to hide under my comforter and cry, but then, I remember - I was called because I am willing, not because I am perfect. God will trade your ashes for beauty if only you will let Him. He will redeem what you broke and turn it into a blessing. He will give you a place to talk about Him and the work He has done in your life if you will surrender and say, "I'm a mess without You. Wanna help a sister out?"

This study is my gift to you. God told me very shortly after my trip to write this. He gave me the word, "abide." I journaled it, prayed about it, and studied what the word truly meant. In John 5, Jesus is speaking to His disciples before He is put to death. He tells them that whoever abides in Him will bear much fruit. When we put our complete dependence in God, we can't help but exude the fruits of the Spirit. The biggest key to abiding is connection. When we are connected to the Lord, we are one with Him and His love flows out of us. In much the same way, when you abide (connect, depend, unite) with your friends, you have a deep soul connection with them. This is the kind of friendship that we are created for. God created us to connect with other people, to hold each other's arms in prayer when they are too weak (Exodus 17:12). This study is not a boastful "I am so wonderful and amazing, and you should do what I say" kind of study. This is a "here's how I've screwed up and here's how God redeemed it" study. Learn from my mistakes, and be better for it.

___+++___

Oh, Jesus, Jesus, Jesus. Thank You for turning my ashes into beauty. Thank You for fixing the things that I screwed up. Thank You for being the author and finisher of my faith. Your story is the only one I want my life to follow.

Lord, bless each woman who reads this study, and may You speak to her heart in the exact way she needs it. I pray wisdom and insight over each woman. Use my words to speak into their lives so that they may learn from my mistakes, rather than make these mistakes themselves.

Open our hearts, our minds, and our eyes to be more like You and less like us. Because You're way cooler than we are.

Amen

——DAY TWO——

Companionship

If you ask any married woman, she will likely tell you that she's not sure what her husband would do without her. Would he be able to feed himself? Would he lock the doors at night? Could he even attempt to start a load of laundry? We joke that our men need us to perform basic human functions, but I don't think it's a coincidence that in the second passage of the first book of the Bible, God tells us that it is not good for man(kind) to be alone. Right off the bat, Genesis 2:18 tells us that it is best to do life with a helper.

Now, granted, this passage is speaking about a husband and wife team, but I think it speaks to our entire lives. How much better is a Target run with a girlfriend? How much better is it to celebrate job promotions, proposals, and pregnancy announcements surrounded by friends who love you? And on the flip side, how much deeper is your friendship when you experience great loss? Do you have that girlfriend who will bring you your favorite kind of chai and trashy magazines when you are laid up from a gut-wrenching miscarriage? Doesn't she sound like someone you want in your life? She does. If we are completely honest with ourselves, our heart is aching for her—for them. In your darkest moments, wouldn't it have been less dark with a girlfriend stroking your hair, ordering pizza, and putting on a Sandra Bullock movie?

Do you know why you feel that way? Because the Lord made you that way. He made you for companionship. He gave you that desire to have friends who love and care for you because He loves and cares for us.

Then the Lord said, It is not good that the man should be alone. I will make him a helper fit for him.
Genesis 2:18 ESV

Have you found your tribe? Who are they? Write their names below.

Maybe you are reading this and the ache for girlfriends is becoming deeper. Here's where you take your heart to God. Tell Him your desire. Psalm 37:4 says that when we take delight in Him, He is faithful to give us the desires of your heart. Girl, He knows the desires of your heart because He created you. He wants you to tell Him, to lean on Him, to trust Him, and to confide in Him. He already knows you and loves you more deeply than you could ever understand. Talk to Him like you would your girlfriend. He's listening.

COMPANIONSHIP

Thank You, Almighty Father, for knowing exactly what we need before even we know it. Thank You for the helpers and friends in our lives we get to share the ups and downs with. And most of all, Jesus, thank You doesn't even begin to cover what our relationship with You means.

Make us feel Your presence right this second. Wrap Your arms around each woman reading this and let her know that You are right there with her. Thank You for never leaving us alone.

Amen

——DAY THREE——

Create

I make friends easily. I like to joke around, make people laugh, and make people feel completely at ease. I want to feel comfortable around you, so if I break the ice, more than likely, we can be buddies within a few minutes of meeting each other.

On the other hand, I know many women who do not feel the same way I do. There are many reasons behind this, which we will not get into, but you know the women I'm talking about. Maybe some of you are that woman. Maybe you are completely uncomfortable with meeting new people, and consequently, you clam up in these kinds of settings.

I'm going to let you in on a secret: There is something inside of all of us that is scared of rejection. We are scared to make a joke because someone might think it's stupid. We are scared to introduce ourselves because the woman we just met definitely has her life put together, and your life is about as frayed as the bottom of your well-loved yoga pants. 2 Timothy

1:7 tells us that God didn't make us fear-filled—He empowered us with love.

You've heard the phrase: your vibe attracts your tribe. It's entirely true. My vibe is funny, silly, light-hearted, and fun. The women closest to me are funny, silly, light-hearted, and fun. Funny how that worked, huh? What you put out to the masses—whether purposely or not—is what you attract. If you go to a social function and spend your time in the corner with your arms crossed, you aren't really going to attract people. Now, when you walk into your Bible study or a friend's house and you are warm and friendly, people will be drawn to you.

Hear me on this. I am not telling you to be someone you are not. If you are an introvert, own that. If you are an extrovert, own that. What I am telling you is that putting your best foot forward will attract people to you. Be kind, be relatable, and be easy to spend time with. Maybe you aren't a conversation-starter, but you can be a conversation-participator. And if need be, grab your Sharpie and write out 2 Timothy 1:7 on your forearm and chant it over and over until you feel the power and love and sound mind that God gave you.

God gave us a spirit not of fear, but of power and love and sound mind.
2 Timothy 1:7 ESV

Are you an introvert or an extrovert?

How has that affected your relationships in the past?

What is the vibe you create around yourself? Ask the Lord to show you.

Jesus, thank You for making us different. Thank You that there are groups of moms who get dressed head-to-toe everyday, and thank You for the moms who are running to the bus stop in their robes. You created each of us so uniquely, and what a fun Where's Waldo experience it is trying to find the group we fit into.

God, I ask that you would speak to each woman today. Show her who she is in You, and then, help guide her to her tribe. Show her where she fits in this world so that she can feel at home and eventually be able to lead other women. Thank You, Jesus, that we are all puzzle pieces, who—when we are all operating as who You created us to be—come together to create one giant, beautiful puzzle. Guide our missing pieces to us—we miss them.

Amen

——DAY FOUR——

Confidence

Girl A: I have great hair. I have a fun personality. I am really good at writing. I am called.

Girl B: My butt is too big. My eyebrows are shaped weird. I have a crooked nose. I'm too screwed up to be called.

Now, which girl do you want to be friends with? Girl A knows that she has flaws, but those are not what she greets you with. Girl B has been made too aware of her flaws and leads with them. Would you be surprised to hear that Girl A and Girl B are the same person? Would you be surprised to hear that I am both of them?

Let's be really honest here: Sometimes our hormones will dictate which girl we will be from day to day. The definition of confidence is the state of feeling certain about the truth of something. Where does true confidence come from? True confidence comes from being rooted in the Lord and His

Word where He tells us over and over again who we are in Him.

John 1:12 says we are children of God.

Colossians 2:10 says we have been brought to fullness, meaning you lack nothing.

Jeremiah 1:5 says that before God formed you in the womb, He knew you. Before you were born, He set you apart.

Ephesians 1:4 says you are holy and without blame.

And those are only four truths about you. Imagine if you said these verses aloud each day. Would the size of your butt matter anymore? If you were rooted in the true confidence of who God calls you to be, would you really give a rip about how many times you had screwed up? Or would you stand tall and be proud of the times you missed the mark so that God could redeem you?

So, looking at these two girls, who would you like to be friends with? Wouldn't having a girlfriend like Girl A be a breath of fresh air each day? Wouldn't her confidence likely rub off on you? Wouldn't you be encouraged daily by her confidence in who God has called her to be?

James 3:9–12 tells us that Girl A and Girl B can't coexist inside of us. You cannot bless yourself while cursing yourself. When you actively treat yourself like the woman that God knows you are, you will rock that confidence each day. And

CONFIDENCE

I'm telling you what, girl, you will have girls lining up around the block to be your friend because you can't help but contain the love of Jesus inside of you. They will all want Who you have.

You have been made complete in Him.
Colossians 2:10 NIV

What attracts you to certain people? Is it their clothes, their personality, their confidence? Write down the qualities you admire and are attracted to.

Do you exude those qualities? If you answered no, do you actively seek out who you were created to be?

Spend some time asking the Lord to tell you who He created you to be. Ask Him to give you two words that He would use to describe you. Journal about that conversation here.

ANDREA LEBEAU

I am complete in You, Jesus! I am made whole in You! Father, remind us of these truths daily. Remind us that (wo)man's opinion of us is fleeting, but that Your opinion is the only one that matters. Give us the kind of confidence that attracts people to us so that we can shine bright for You. Give us the confidence we need to boldly talk about You. Give us the confidence we need to reach the hurting and the lost.

Forgive us, Lord, when we speak ill of ourselves. Forgive us for believing that we aren't good enough because we aren't a size 2. Forgive us for abusing our bodies in the name of being skinny. And forgive us, oh, Lord, for not thanking You each day for healthy bodies that carry us around, birth babies, feed babies, and keep our families moving and flowing because of how wonderfully we are made. We thank You for what You have given us. Thank You that our thighs touch—our cell phones never fall in the toilet. Thank You that our butts are big—we have a womanly shape. Thank You for every curve and imperfection because that's exactly how You wanted us to be—perfect in Your eyes.

Amen

—— DAY FIVE ——

Support

Are you a good friend? If you sent out an anonymous survey to your 10 closest friends, what would they say about your level of support? Are you a fair-weather friend or an in-the-trenches friend?

I've been both. Like I said in the beginning, I can rock the heck out of a basket of goodies when you are getting a tooth pulled or when you didn't get the promotion you wanted. I've also been the friend who bolted when the situation was too sticky and the decisions weren't clear-cut. I tend to want to problem-solve, and that isn't always easy when faced with some of the hardest situations in life. Those decisions aren't always black or white, A or B, or heads or tails. Those kinds of decisions take time, prayer, and careful consideration.

Patience is something I lack. There. I said it. I'm a move or get out of the way kind of person. I want to get things done. I can tell you truly that a lack of patience and friendship do not mix. There will be times that the answer is wait, and for those of you who are Type-A like me, waiting will feel like fingernails on a chalkboard. Your insides will be screaming, make a decision! Listen to me when I say: Do not act on that impatience. Do not throw the towel in because the wait is too long or the answer is not the one you would have chosen. Support your friends. Pray over them, pray with them. Offer suggestions when asked, but never without provocation. Sit and listen. And when you feel like your ears might bleed, listen some more. I can guarantee that what they are debating in their own heart and mind is much more painful than your lack of patience.

Maybe this chapter is written entirely for myself. I pray that you are a much better friend than I used to be. I pray that you are never in a situation like I was in. Support can look a million different ways, so you have to decide what a healthy amount of support looks like for you and your family. And sometimes, as much as we don't want to admit it, support looks like stepping away for a while. Sometimes the boundary for us lies in backing away and letting our friend work through things. Ecclesiastes 3:5 tells us that there are seasons in our lives where we experience loss and gain.

A friend shows his friendship at all times -it is for adversity that [such] a sister is born.
Proverbs 17:17 CJB

Let's go back to my first questions: Are you a good friend? If

SUPPORT

you sent out an anonymous survey to your 10 closest friends, what would they say about your level of support?

Journal about a time in your life when your girlfriend supported you no matter what. How did that change the situation you were facing?

Spend some time asking the Lord to make you this kind of girlfriend. What does that look like?

Forgive us, Father, where we have fallen short as a friend. Forgive us for making relationships about us and not about loving our friends.

Jesus, fill us with the love that You have. Give us the patience to walk through the processes and support our friends in good and bad times, in sickness and health. Give us long-suffering to be faithful friends. Thank You for being the ultimate example of faithfulness so that we can model it in our own lives.

Amen

—— DAY SIX ——

Cultivate

For all intents and purposes, let's say that you have found your tribe. You are in with a group of women who are good people, enjoyable to be around, and who lift you up. You are blessed, girl!

Now, what are you doing to cultivate these friendships? What are you doing to ensure that there is equal give and take in your relationships?

Let me a paint a visual for you. You and your girls have made it out of the house for a few hours one night for dinner and drinks without husbands or kids. You instantly feel the stress leave your body. You put on makeup, that cute new top, and you don't have baby spit-up anywhere on your body. You look hot! You have been dying to get to this restaurant for a glass of wine and to just talk about everything and nothing with your girlfriends. Drinks and dinner are ordered, and you haven't gotten a single word in because one of your friends has

25

monopolized the entire conversation. It's a story you've heard time and time again with no change, but she has to complain about it over and over. What your friends didn't know is that you found a weird spot on your chest, and you are headed in for a biopsy next week. You were planning to share this very scary, very private news with them during dinner, but there was no opportunity to share.

You now walk away feeling scared, unsupported, and probably pretty annoyed that your friend couldn't stop complaining. Your friend was entirely selfish, and as a result, she shut down your opportunity to share a very important, potentially life-altering moment in your life.

Don't be that friend. Ask your friends how they are doing. Cultivate an atmosphere of sharing. Cultivate a safe space that you can all share in, where each person feels heard and understood. The fastest way to close those friendships up for good is by making someone feel unseen. There is nothing wrong with sharing what you are going through, but be sure to cultivate an atmosphere where everyone has space to share. Philippians 4:5 calls us to be considerate in everything that we do.

Romans 14 talks about cultivating good relationships. Don't get caught up in the minutia of day-to-day life. Be kind, love each other, support each other. That's it. Everything else is just icing.

But the fruit of the Spirit [the result of His presence within us] is love [unselfish concern for others], joy, [inner] peace,

CULTIVATE

patience [not the ability to wait, but how we act while waiting], kindness, goodness, faithfulness, gentleness, self-control. Against such things there is no law.
Galatians 5:22–23 AMP

How does it make you feel when you have something important to share, and you aren't given the opportunity? Now, how do you think others feel when they don't get their chance to share?

Lord, we thank You for the way you are all-inclusive with each one of us. You don't favor one over the other, and because of that, we can come to You at all hours of the day and talk to You. Thank You for this give and take relationship. Thank You for speaking to me when I need to hear Your voice, and then, listening to me when I need to unburden my heart. You are the ultimate Friend. Teach me to be a friend just like You. Open my heart wider to include more friends.

Amen

——DAY SEVEN——

Adult Friends

Let's dispel a myth quickly: Most adult women do not have lifelong friends who have known them since they were toddling. If you have that, you are a rarity, and we're all jealous of you. No, most of us moved away after high school or college, got jobs, got married, started families, and are just trying to keep our heads above water. Cultivating friendships seems like a lot of effort, and sweatpants are typically discouraged when meeting new people, so we opt out.

However, I'm guessing if you haven't found your tribe, you may be enjoying your sweats in the comfort of your own home, but your heart is aching for connection, right? You may think you are doing just fine, but at the end of the day, you are tired of cleaning up crackers, breaking up fights, and refilling sippy cups. Your soul is craving a deeper connection. Well, if we look back at Genesis 2:18, we know that that longing is because we are created for connection. But, girl, I get it: It is hard to meet other women. Where do you meet other women who need friends? Likely, you'll see a woman at the park with her kids, and assume that she already has her fill of friends and doesn't have time to add another.

I will tell you that it is hard to meet new friends. As a child, if you both rocked some cool leggings, that was it—you were best friends. Being an adult and making friends is so much harder. How do you know what other people like? Are you ready for the answer? You. ask. them. Being vulnerable is one of the hardest things in life that we can do. Letting down our walls that protect us is a really tall order. But what if I told you that what you are feeling isn't foreign to many women? What if I told you that we all crave the same kind of connection because that is the way that God made each and every one of us? What if I told you that you could have a large circle of really amazing friends if you simply struck up a conversation here and there? I can feel the introverts cringing and throwing this book across the room. Let me be honest: I'm an extrovert, and that thought still makes my palms sweaty. It is not easy to make friends with strangers, and I would never tell you it is.

However, I think if we are honest with ourselves, we could truthfully say that the friendships we've made as adults came from situations where either you or your friend asked a simple question, and one of you squeaked out a "me too!" and the rest was history. That's all it takes. You find common ground. "I like Target. You like Target. We'd probably be good friends." 2 Corinthians 12:9 tells us that His power is made perfect in our weakness. That moment when you let your walls down, there is so much power in your vulnerability because the Lord is able to use you to reach other women. YOU. He wants to use you to reach women who need friends. If we can only reverse our thinking and stop feeling like we are the only ones who feel alone, we could impact the world in a huge way. Instead of waiting for other people to reach us, let's reach others who need US. Remember, you and I are puzzle pieces that all fit together, so when we are missing our pieces, our masterpiece is incomplete.

But He said to me, "My grace is sufficient for you, for my power is made perfect in weakness." Therefore I will boast all the more gladly of my weaknesses, so that the power of Christ may rest upon me.
2 Corinthians 12:9 NLT

What keeps you from striking up conversations with new people?

How would you act differently if you knew that your vulnerability would be accepted, and it would form a connection?

Can you think of women who need the same connection you

crave? Write their names down and ask the Lord to open doors that allow you to connect with them.

⟡

Father, you created us for community. We are not complete without others. Please help us see that just because we feel like we're doing ok without friends that it would be so much sweeter and so much more fulfilling when we find our true connection.

Show us, Lord, what true vulnerability looks like. Teach us to use the good, bad, and ugly to connect with other women. Lord, break down barriers that would have us believe that other women have their lives more together than we do. We know deep down that it isn't true, so help us to believe it. And show us, God, that we do not have to have everything in order to be the best kind of friend. Thank you that You use our imperfections to further Your Kingdom. Thank You that we are not perfect so that we have to rely on You each and every day.

Amen

—DAY EIGHT—

Seasons

If the song Turn! Turn! Turn! isn't playing in your head, lucky you. This song will probably play on repeat in my head for months.

This chapter is a little touchy, but I hope you will be open to understanding my heart and experiences. Ecclesiastes 3:6 tells us that there is a season for everything: a time to seek and a time to lose, a time to keep, and a time to cast away. This chapter in Ecclesiastes can be so hard to read because Solomon is telling us that there will be good and bad in life. You will love people, and they will die. You will laugh, and you will cry. Life is going to throw you the good, bad, and ugly. The bad and the ugly will at times be the loss of a friendship.

At 29 years old, I had had one daughter and six pregnancies. My body wasn't cooperating. If you know anything about secondary infertility, you know that it is nothing short of excruciating. You had a child before - why can't you do it again? I was poked, prodded, swabbed, scraped, pricked, examined, and tested. I could get pregnant, but I couldn't stay pregnant. I know what every single twinge in my body means. I'd wake up and know that if I grabbed a pregnancy test, it would read positive. I also knew that if that test was positive, two weeks later, it would read negative. My body was tired and frustrated. I was failing as a woman. I couldn't do the one thing that a woman should be able to do: create and carry a baby.

After a long day at a wedding, my very best friend in the whole world was out of town, but I had borrowed her truck and had to take it back. I let myself into the house, grabbed a cold beer out of her fridge, and dialed her number. I sat on her couch and sobbed uncontrollably. This was it: This was the last time we were trying. I couldn't take it any longer, and once again, it wasn't happening. During that cycle, I had taken Clomid (a medication my OB/GYN prescribed that stimulates ovulation), but I just knew I wasn't pregnant. She quickly told me that that was stupid and to go to her bathroom and grab a test she had way back in the cabinet.

Positive.

My tears quickly dried up, and I placed the unopened beer back in the fridge. We squealed and cried and laughed at what a drama queen I had been.

The following months were the most trying of my life: I was not only pregnant, but I was also carrying twins. Being that I had had so many miscarriages, I was high-risk and now there were two buns in my oven. I spent nearly my entire pregnancy on bedrest, followed by hospital bedrest when I went into labor at 27 weeks. Don't worry: I kept those baby boys nice and comfortable until 35 weeks!

My best friend was there through everything: loss, fear, bedrest, birth, NICU time, exhaustion. We joked that we would end up spending our last days together in a nursing home once our husbands had passed. That wasn't our story.

Our incredible friendship was a chapter in both of our books. We stood by each other for really good and really bad times. We loved each other, we fought with each other, we made each other laugh, we made each other cry. Things shifted in both of our lives and without any pomp and circumstance, our friendship shifted as well. I thank God everyday for who she was and who she is now. The woman that I loved so deeply will have a piece of my heart forever, and I know that our chapter together brought me to the next chapter, and I hope I did the same for her.

For everything there is a season, and a time for every matter under heaven:
a time to be born, and a time to die;
a time to plant, and a time to pluck up what is planted;
a time to kill, and a time to heal;
a time to break down, and a time to build up;
a time to weep, and a time to laugh;
a time to mourn, and a time to dance;
a time to cast away stones, and a time to gather stones together;

SEASONS

a time to embrace, and a time to refrain from embracing;
a time to seek, and a time to lose;
a time to keep, and a time to cast away;
a time to tear, and a time to sew;
a time to keep silence, and a time to speak;
a time to love, and a time to hate;
a time for war, and a time for peace.
Ecclesiastes 3:1-8 ESV

Loss is always hard, but sometimes it can be such a beautiful thing when you see why the loss is necessary. Yes, there are seasons where you will mourn, but girlfriend, your season of dancing is just around the corner.

Have you ever experienced the loss of a dear friend?

⤙✦

Father God, thank You for the seasons in our lives. Thank You that we can taste the bad so that we can truly enjoy the good. Lord, when we experience the lows and the losses, come alongside us and reassure us that You never leave us. Thank You, God, for the tears, because we know that the laughter is right around the corner.

Amen

—DAY NINE—

Bad Apples

I love to have fun! I don't like to be too serious, and if
a conversation is leaning that way, I chime in with a joke.
Comedic timing is part of my heritage. I am drawn to people
who laugh all the time, who have joy radiating out of their
pores, and who enjoy life. I think that's a given: Most people
aren't drawn to the Eeyore's of the world. The most attractive
people are the ones who are fun, positive, and joyful.

These are all amazing characteristics to have, but if you
aren't careful, you can wind up with girlfriends who are only
fun. These are the friends you can go out with and enjoy
your time with, but these are typically not the friends who
are going to do much for your spiritual edification. Believe it
or not, there is a balance out there. 1 Corinthians 15:33 tells
us that bad girlfriends can bring out the worst in us.

I think it's safe to say that we have all had one or more
friends who really didn't do much in bringing out the best in

us. That's okay because God's grace is deep and wide, and He will use that to help you in the future. Maybe the lesson is seeing who you are in Christ apart from those friends or even seeing the contrast between women who edify you and the friends who don't do all that much for your character development. I've been on both sides of that coin, and the great thing is that I get to use the experiences I've had and make better choices. Plus, I get to tell you how I've screwed up with the hope that you'll learn from my mistakes! Win–win! Proverbs 13:20 tells us that when we choose friends wisely, they will rub off on us. Use discernment in choosing your friends, and you will build each other up and not tear each other down.

Be encouraged! I have an amazing group of women friends who make me laugh until I nearly pee and who will carry my deepest heartache with me. These kind of girlfriends are definitely out there, and likely, they are just waiting until you come along to complete their friendship circle.

Whoever walks with the wise becomes wise, but the companion of fools will suffer him.
Proverbs 13:20 NASB

Take inventory of your friendships. Identify the women in your life who build you up. Write their names below and pray a prayer of blessing over them.

Now ask the Lord to open your eyes to any friendships that

need pruning in your life. Be honest with Him, and He will reveal truth to you.

⸎

God, thank You for the gift of discernment. Open our eyes to examine the friends we have surrounding us right now. Help us to make wise choices in who we spend our time with. I ask, Lord, that You would give us wisdom when choosing those who are closest to us. Bring women into our lives who edify us, who are kind, loving, and who add to our lives and not subtract. Thank You for Your hand in all we do and say.

Amen

──DAY TEN──

Forgiveness

I'll be honest with you: There was a lull in writing because of a situation of unforgiveness in my life. I didn't think I could write about friendship or forgiveness when I was walking through it, but I know that the reason I am writing this now is because He's telling me to.

I think our biggest stumbling block is that we want forgiveness and grace in our own lives, but when we are wronged, we want our offender to get what they have coming to them. Be grateful God is God and we are not in charge of handing out grace and forgiveness. 2 Corinthians 5:17 says that we are new women in Christ. When we tell Jesus we messed up and ask His forgiveness, He removes our sins as far as the east is from the west (Psalm 103:12). Now, make a woman mad, and you'll want to sit down, tuck your head between your knees, and brace for impact!

The key thing to remember about unforgiveness is that

it is entirely a matter of the heart. Let's say your friend has wronged you. You wake up mad, call your other friends in your "righteous anger," tell the clerk at the post office, call your mom to let her know what has happened, stand over the stove while you cook dinner with your anger seeping out of your pores, complain about it over dinner, and then, go to bed angry.

What has your anger done for your friend? Nothing. You wasted an entire day being mad and offended, and likely, she was blissfully unaware of your anger and probably had a fun day not harboring bitterness, resentment, and anger. You have now spent days working on your future wrinkles.

You love your friend, but she messed up. Colossians 3:13 tells us to work through our issues with our friends and then forgive them. That's your job. You forgive, and you move on. Now, if this friend is a repeat offender,and it's not a healthy relationship, refer back to the last chapter.

The next time you are weighing a situation where you have been offended, I want you to think about something: If you had been the offender and not the offended, how would you want to be treated? How would you want your friend to respond to you? In kindness and mercy? Or in anger and rage? Forgiveness is less about the person who wrongs you and more about your own heart. Forgive more freely, and you'll wrinkle more slowly.

Be tolerant with each other and, if someone has a complaint against anyone, forgive each other. As the Lord forgave you,

FORGIVENESS

so also forgive each other.
Colossians 3:13 CEB

If there is any unforgiveness in your heart right now, lay it down. Tell your heart story below, and then, release it the Lord.

Have you wronged anyone and not apologized? Dig deep and see if there is anything you need to be forgiven for.

Sometimes we aren't even aware of the unforgiveness we are harboring in our hearts. Take some time to ask the Lord to reveal any unforgiveness or bitterness hiding in your heart. When He shows you, lay it at His feet and feel the overwhelming power of forgiveness.

Father, forgive us for being unforgiving at times. Forgive us for being selfish in our quest for grace and mercy and for being slow to give it to those around us. We lay our offenses at Your feet and ask for a complete cleansing. Fill us with Your love, which binds everything together in perfect harmony. Help us to be more like You each day, Lord.

Amen

—DAY ELEVEN—

I Got You, Babe

At twenty-seven weeks pregnant with twin boys, I was in active labor. I was sent an hour away to a hospital that was equipped for preterm births. Only, this is what happened: I got to the hospital, where I was hooked up to monitors and pumped full of medications to stop labor. It was a depressing and frustrating 48 hours, but it worked! The boys were safe and sound, and I remained in the hospital for six full weeks of rest.

For a woman who struggled with anxiety for many years, this looming hospital stay seemed like a form of torture. My sister and I will frequently call each other for no reason, and say, "Talk to me! I can't be alone with my thoughts!" We have anxiety and jokes, folks! I envisioned padded walls and utter silence.

What I was not expecting was to have visitors nearly everyday, bringing lunch, Starbucks, magazines, and books.

In those six weeks, there were only four days when I didn't have a visitor. God provided in an incredible way that I didn't even really see at the time. I was over an hour away from our hometown, which meant visitors were taking time out of their day to sit on the interstate for a couple of hours and then sit in a hospital room with me just because I was stuck there. I was unable to care for my daughter, and her grandparents stepped in and took over. The phrase "it takes a village" defines that entire season of my life.

This is what we are created for. This is how we are the hands and feet of Jesus. This is how we spread His love to others. Galatians 6:2 tells us to bear each other's burdens. When your friend needs help, step in. If we go back to Genesis 2:18 where God clearly points out that we are made for community, then it's an easy jump to see where we need to be there in the good and bad times with our friends. When you're walking through a difficult time, wouldn't it be easier if your friends did some of the heavy lifting for you?

Be her. Be the friend who is reliable and dependable with the small things. Show yourself as faithful. You never know when you might need some burden–bearing friends to come alongside in a time of need.

Bear one another's burdens, and so fulfill the law of Christ.
Galatians 6:2 ESV

Has there ever been a time in your life when you needed your community to rally around you? Has there ever been a time in your friend's lives when they needed you to rally around them?

Did you do it?

Write down some ways you can be the hands and feet of Jesus to the women in your life, and I dare you to put those ways into action this week!

꧁

Jesus, we thank You for the gift of community. Thank You for creating us with a need to be connected and to do life with others. God, give us opportunities to bear our friends' burdens. Help us to be faithful in those moments - to make the long drives, to give up some of our alone time - when our friends need us the most. And Jesus, surround each woman reading this with friends who will do the same for her. Place the right friends in her life to walk through the hard things together.

Amen

——DAY TWELVE——

Gossip

"Raise your hand if you have been personally victimized by Regina George." If you have never seen Mean Girls, put down this study and turn on Netflix.

How many of you have met a Regina George at some point in your life? Ok, you can put your hands down. We all have. We all know someone whose entire world is gossip. We all know someone whose goal is to turn friends on each other. Maybe you've been that friend. Proverbs 16:28 tells us that a whisperer separates close friends. Those moments when you've just shared a simple secret is how the enemy pits us against each other to ultimately separate us.

Honestly, I have been Regina George more often than I care to admit. If you asked my peers to raise their hands if they've been personally victimized by me, there would be a lot of hands raised. My girlfriend and I had a discussion a few weeks ago about a time in our lives when we wanted to be envied.

ANDREA LEBEAU

But why? James 4 tells us because, as humans, our drive to get ahead pits us against each other. If you get ahead, it means that, in some way, I come up short.

Ephesians 4:25–32 implores us to be kind, to speak only what is true, and to build each other up. If we spend our time swapping stories about other people, what have we gained? Do you feel better when you say things about your friends to your other friends? Proverbs 27:9 says that a good friend refreshes the soul and brings life. When we spend our time sharing secrets, we are doing the opposite. We share with our friends because we need counsel and someone to share our burdens. How much deeper would our friendships be if we understood the weight of that truth? How much more would we value the times when our girlfriends let their guards down to reveal their true hearts? How much more would we tuck those vulnerabilities away and protect them?

If nothing else sticks, remember that Proverbs 11:13 tells us that if she gossips with you, she'll gossip about you. When your friend reveals her secrets to you, bring light and life in those instances. Counsel her, pray with her, and put those secrets in the vault (James 5:12).

...a sweet friendship refreshes the soul.
Proverbs 27:9 MSG

How has gossip negatively affected your friendships?

GOSSIP

I'm going to ask you to dig a little deeper here. Think of an instance when you gossiped to a friend. What was the root of your gossip?

Take some time and ask the Lord to reveal the times you gossiped. Lay them at His feet and ask Him to give you a spirit of unity with your friends.

_ﷻ_

Lord, we ask Your forgiveness for the times we have gossiped. Whatever the reasoning, it was wrong, and we know that. God, give us a deeper understanding of what true friendship means. Show us the kind of friend You intended us to be. Make us be the kind of friend who refreshes our friends' souls and creates unity—not division.

Thank You for the friendships You have given us. Help us to treasure them more deeply.

Amen

——DAY THIRTEEN——

Therapy

I never really thought about it this way, but we have built-in therapists. The more I started to study the Word and what it says about friendship, the more I realized that as friends, we are called to be counselors. And the best part about that is that friends are free!

Some of my favorite nights involve my girlfriends gathered around my kitchen island. We like to eat, drink, and be merry, and my glaringly obvious spiritual gift is hospitality. Give me a boring, old week night, and I will have my kitchen filled with music, laughter, and my favorite women. What is so special about every one of those nights is that at some point, with mouths full of cookie dough, guards are dropped. There is a level of comfort and safety created during those times that allows each of us to share. Proverbs 12:26 says in an abundance of counselors, there is safety. That safety is created when we get together.

What is so special about these nights that women feel at ease to share? Nothing. The invitation was simply to come over, bake cookies, and sip wine. I truly believe that Matthew 18:20 is played out constantly when believers are together. We may not be gathering for Bible study, but we are together, we love Jesus, and we love each other. Our spirits are connected, and those are the moments when we are able to share how our kids are driving us crazy, how we are struggling financially, or how we feel inadequate in every area of our lives.

That's the magic sauce to creating that level of comfort: Love God (Deuteronomy 6:5), listen to His counsel (Proverbs 2:6), and choose friends who do the same (Proverbs 13:20). On days three and six, we talked about creating and cultivating fcultivating environments where friendships can thrive. I'm going to ask you again to act out these ideas.

Gather your friends together for a game night, bake cookies, or even head to Starbucks for an hour to spend time together. If you aren't an events organizer, head to your church, and find a group of women who love Jesus. I will tell you that it may take some time to find the right group, but I promise you that that group exists. Ask God to point you in the right direction. And if God doesn't answer right away, remember that He took a couple of years to answer my prayer for friendship. Let that encourage you—that He is painting your masterpiece even when you don't see it.

For where two or three gather together as my followers, I am there among them.
Matthew 18:20 NLT

Think about the times in your life when you felt most comfortable with your friends. What were the elements that made you feel at ease? What was the atmosphere like?

It's your turn to cultivate some of that magic sauce. Look at your calendar, text your girlfriends, and make a plan to get together. It doesn't have to be fancy or formal, but it does need to happen. Grab a cheap bottle of wine, some prepackaged cookie dough, and spend some time together. Play a game or do nothing, but spend some time together.

God, thank You for Your wise counsel. Thank You that we have Your Word to follow day in and day out. Thank You for speaking to us each day. Lord, give us opportunities to create a safe space for our friends. Let us be the safety net that our friends need to let down their guard. Help us to offer wise counsel and surround them with love in those moments. Help us to be the kind of friend You are to us.

Amen

—DAY FOURTEEN—

Gather

When God first gave me the vision for this study, He showed me a picture of a farmhouse table. It was long, maybe 20 women were gathered around it, and it was full of food, beautiful place settings, and so much laughter. The Hallmark Channel could not have created such a beautiful vision of love and friendship. Naturally, when God speaks to me, He speaks in my language: a home filled with people I love.

I can look back on my childhood and see how this feeling of hospitality was developed. My grandparents lived in a small home for a large portion of my life, and my very favorite holidays were filled with laughter, some yelling, some sketchy food, and my family. We'd pack ourselves into that living room with our plates on our laps and just be. We were loud, we were obnoxious, and we were fun. Those holidays in that tiny living room are some of my favorite memories. The house was nothing to speak of, but that didn't matter. As Walt Whitman pointed out, "We were together, I forget the rest."

Even as a small child, the gift of hospitality that God gave me was being nurtured and cultivated in our family get-togethers. I came across a passage in Acts 2 a while ago that stood out to me. We see something called the fellowship of the believers laid out so beautifully in verses 42–47. The Apostles have come together, dedicating themselves to the Lord and to each other. They did everything together—they went to church together, ate together, praised the Lord together, and had favor with people. Then, day by day, God would send more people to them to be saved. This passage perfectly depicted the vision of the farmhouse table. Here were a group of best friends who loved God and loved each other, being the hands and feet of Jesus.

Just a few weeks before writing this, my vision became reality during a book club gathering at my house. With 20 women packed around our farmhouse table and around our island, God whispered, "Look at what's happening." I stepped back, took a photo, and the tears welled up in my eyes. My heart was full. Not only had I seen God's vision so clearly and heard His voice, but also He was fulfilling this vision just weeks after He had shown me His call on my life.

It is no coincidence that one of the most important passages in the Bible depicts Jesus eating with His closest friends in the world before His death. Have you ever thought about that? The act of sitting down to dinner together, breaking bread, and being together is one of the most famous depictions in history. Yet again, this is God showing us that we are made for community and friendship.

GATHER

Day after day they went to the house of God together. In their houses they ate their food together. Their hearts were happy. They gave thanks to God and all the people respected them. The Lord added to the group each day those who were being saved from the punishment of sin.
Acts 2:46–47 NLV

Your homework for the week is to choose a date, time, and place, and invite some girlfriends to get out for an hour or two. Talk, eat, share, laugh, cry, but just be together.

Lord, thank You for giving us story after story in the Bible about the importance of gathering together. Thank You for the communities that You have given us. Help us not to neglect meeting together and encouraging each other (Hebrews 10:25).

For those without this community, God we ask for Your provision. Thank You that You have the perfect community for each of us, and I ask that You would lead each woman to her perfect place. And Lord, for those of us who have that community, I ask that you give us a spirit of inclusion. Make us into women who draw other women into community and into a safe place.

Amen

—DAY FIFTEEN—

Pray

I have this friend named Brittany. I would say that we call each other no less than five times per day. I have a thought, and I need to run it by Brittany. What I love about Brittany is that she is very wise, very insightful, and loves Jesus. I trust what she has to say because she is rocking the Jesus connection daily.

Shortly after I came back from my business conference, I was movin' and groovin'. God was opening doors left and right, I was seeing the fruits of some seeds I had planted over the past few months, and I knew that I had been called to minister to women. I had very clearly seen the vision of the farmhouse table filled with women. I happened to share this with someone in our church who didn't think that I was hearing God very clearly. I was crushed. I knew that I had heard from God, and I knew what He had shown me, but because she was a trusted leader, she was right, and I was clearly wrong.

I immediately phoned Brittany—my entire calling was now in question. Brittany's response was, "Well, did you ask the Holy Spirit about it?" I quickly snapped back, "No! I called you!" She told me to chill out and ask God to confirm the word I'd been given. The Lord confirmed it for me, but Brittany was the one who taught me the most valuable lesson in all of that.

The Bible so clearly tells us to pray about everything (Philippians 4:6–7), but I had been confused by the words that God was speaking, so I needed someone on this side of heaven to help clear it up. Not only did I pray and ask God to help, but Brittany also got off the phone and prayed for me. She prayed for clarity and confirmation. The conversation was simple, and her answer was simple, but one we think of as a backup all the time: Pray.

When you have issues in your life, do your girlfriends pray for you? Do you pray for them? Our go-to is to call our girlfriends, and that's normal. YOU are normal! However, what if, instead of just downloading our information, we asked them immediately, "Will you pray with me right now?" I would bet that we would see quicker answers to our prayers, deeper friendships, and so much gossip would be avoided if our first response is to pray with and for our friends. Throughout the New Testament, Paul travels around, speaking to different people, and begins almost all of his letters by telling his friends that he misses them and that he prays for them. Philippians 1:3 opens with Paul telling the Philippians that when he thinks of them, it triggers him to give thanks and to pray for them. This is our model for our

Matthew 18:20 tells us that when two or more believers are together, He's with us. That second you begin praying with your girlfriends, the Holy Spirit is there, listening to your prayers. If we know that we are made for human connection as well as connection to Jesus, can't we make the assumption that marrying the two would develop even deeper heart connections? I triple dog dare you to try that the next time you need your friends' counsel.

Every time you cross my mind, I break out in exclamations of thanks to God. Each exclamation is a trigger to prayer. I find myself praying for you with a glad heart.
Philippians 1:3 MSG

Being very honest with yourself, who do you turn to first in times of need?

Take some time now to talk to the Lord about what is going on in your life. Lay your burdens at His feet. When you have caught Him up on your life, spend some time praying over your friends and their needs.

PRAY

Holy Spirit, thank You for being available to us 24/7. Thank You for being accessible in every moment of our lives. Help us to remember to run to You for counsel when we need it. Remind us that You are the One who can see our future and that You are the One who steers us in the way we should go.

Lord, we thank You for our friends and we ask that You would cover them with grace, wisdom, and protection. When we think of our girlfriends, let it remind us to thank You for them and to pray for them

Amen

—DAY SIXTEEN—

Serve Your Friends

I think it's pretty clear that I love to fill my home with women. I think it's also pretty clear that I love to cook and bake for those people. Combine the two, and I am a happy woman. I truly believe that God gave me the gift of hospitality because of my love for people. The things that I choose for our home are purely driven by how they will function when we have friends over. The music played, the oils diffused, the table settings all help to create the atmosphere when my friends come over. The intention is to make them feel special, welcomed, and at home. As the meal is served, I am sure to serve them first. The natural inclination is to fill my plate before anyone else. I mean, I didn't get this butt by waiting my turn to be served!

There is something so special, however, about watching the fruit of your labor being heaped onto your friends' plates. You have spent time to make them something that they will love, and they are receiving the love that you are serving them. One of the most beautiful verses in the Bible that is underlined, highlighted, and circled is Matthew 20:28 which it tells us that Jesus came to serve people, not to be served. The Son of God, the King of everything came to serve people. He could have easily lounged under a palm tree being waited on hand and foot, but instead, He took to the streets and served the men and women He loved so deeply.

Proverbs 11:25 tells us to be a blessing and that our lives will be enriched. I think what Solomon is telling us is that when we serve people and show them the love of Jesus, our lives will be blessed in all kinds of ways. Opening your home to people is just one way to be the hands and feet of Jesus, but how many times do you gather with your girlfriends, and they wind up speaking truth and goodness into your life? How many times do help someone in need, and it fills your heart in a way that no material good could?

There is power in serving our friends. Acts 20:35 tells us that we are better off giving than receiving. Why do you think that is? I believe it's because there is more to be said of giving ourselves than of being stingy. Jesus came to give everything away - He didn't keep anything for Himself. In that, He gained eternity with the people He loved with all of His heart. It was painful and awful as He gave His life, but His gain was greater. If we take a page out of His book (see what I did there!?), He is telling us that our gain will be greater. We are here to change lives by loving and serving people.

Whatever your gift, use it to serve others. Maybe your calling is not to hospitality, and you know what? That's ok!

wisdom, knowledge, mercy, and administration. You know what? I am absolutely terrible when it comes to those gifts, but that's how it's supposed to be. We are puzzle pieces who make a beautiful work of art when we all work together. Maybe my job is to set the table and make a way for my exhorting friends to begin their work. I am perfectly happy with that because it is who God made me to be. When we are serving together, the puzzle is just as God hoped it would: beautiful.

Be generous with the different things God gave you, passing them around so all get in on it: if words, let it be God's words; if help, let it be God's hearty help. That way, God's bright presence will be evident in everything through Jesus, and he'll get all the credit as the One mighty in everything—encores to the end of time.
1 Peter 4:10–11 MSG

I want you to take a few minutes and ask God to reveal your spiritual gifts to you. If you are at a loss, jump online and find a spiritual gifts test. This was such a great tool for me in pinpointing the gifts and talents God gave me.

What are your spiritual gifts, and how can you use them to serve your friends and family?

SERVE YOUR FRIENDS

Jesus, thank You for the wisdom You have in creating us each so uniquely. Thank You that we are not all the same. Thank You that when we operate in our talents and gifts, You are faithful to use our strengths to bless those around us. Thank You for the puzzle pieces that all fit together.

Lord, I ask that you would reveal each woman's gifts and talents to her. Show her how perfectly you made her. Show her how her gifts are necessary and perfect to create this work of art. And then, God, give her opportunities to serve. Open doors to serve Your people so that she might see the vision You have for her life.

Amen

—DAY SEVENTEEN—

Communion

I grew up in a Baptist church in southern California. I'm not sure if my church had considered that the New Testament tells us that Jesus is the bread of life and not the wafer of life, but nonetheless, communion was a wafer of Jesus. In all honesty, I loved communion Sunday because it broke up the monotony of listening to the harpist pluck away and the "thou shalt nots" that made up each service.

I will also tell you that, while I loved that we'd get a shot of grape juice mid-service, I was always terrified that if I partook in communion and I didn't have my issues settled with Jesus, I was going to turn into a pillar of salt on that light blue, creaky pew. What I learned in that stained glass building was that you were going to burn if you deigned to eat your wafer and drink your grape juice and you had unconfessed sins.

As I got a little older and started attending a non-denominational church, I learned the value and the beauty of communion not because I was in a different church, but because I grew up a little. Charismatic churches give you a hunk of Jesus and wine. Count me in. If you study the meaning of communion and look back at the Lord's supper, He is telling us to do this to be close to Him. Even Dictionary.com gets the definition of communion better than my old church: the sharing or exchanging of intimate thoughts and feelings, especially when the exchange is on a mental or spiritual level. The act of communion is about being together and being intimate.

Fast forward to this year, one of our Bible study leaders suggested that each time we come together, we should take communion together. I will tell you that there is no shortage of bread or wine at our gatherings, so it's not really a stretch to make this happen. We are after all women and moms.

I admit that the first time we took communion together as a community of women, it gave me pause. It made me look into the meaning of communion before it finally clicked for me. In Luke 22, just before Jesus is sent to death, one of His final acts is sitting around a table with His best friends, eating dinner. He tells them to gather together and take communion as an act of admitting that He is Lord. 1 Corinthians 11 then goes on to tell us that when we gather together, many times, there will be some offenses taken up. Let's be honest: We're women. Attitudes, PMS, bad hair days, and grumpy kids are going to follow us around, but when you gather together with your friends in the name of Jesus, communion tells us to stop and take a moment. This is a time to drop the baggage we carried in with us, to turn our focus to Jesus and our friends,

If you need a good bread recipe, check Pinterest for The Famous New York Times No Knead Bread. You're welcome. Grab a bottle of wine and just before you begin your study or conversation time together, say a quick prayer, acknowledging Jesus and express your thankfulness for the women gathered around you. Then, eat, drink, and be merry!

So, my friends, when you come together to the Lord's Table, be reverent and courteous with one another. If you're so hungry that you can't wait to be served, go home and get a sandwich. But by no means risk turning this Meal into an eating and drinking binge or a family squabble. It is a spiritual meal - a love feast.
1 Corinthians 11:33–34 MSG

Have you ever considered taking communion just before Bible study begins? Does it feel a little awkward?

What have your experiences with communion been like?

Spend some time asking the Lord to reveal His truths and blessings surrounding communion.

COMMUNION

Lord, we thank You for Your death on the cross because it means we get to be with You forever. Thank You for the representation of communion, and the intimacy it creates between us and our friends. As we gather, make Your presence known to each of the women and create a deeper friendship as we take the time to participate in communion.

Amen

—DAY EIGHTEEN—

Love Your Friends

After two miscarriages, I found out I was pregnant just before Christmas 2009. I gave birth to the most beautiful, cone-headed girl Maddie in August 2010. My pregnancy was a breeze, as was her delivery. The curse of miscarriages had been broken! As Maddie neared age two, we decided to try for a sibling. One month later, I was pregnant. Because of my miscarriage history, we were seen right away and given an ultrasound at the same appointment. It was a blob, but it was a beautiful blob with a strong heartbeat. Deep breath.

That summer, we had family from out-of-town visiting, so we spent a week taking them to the various sites in Colorado. One evening, we decided to stay home. Oddly enough, I remember so vividly that we sat watching the Olympics on TV together.

Without any warning at 11 weeks pregnant, the cramps started to wash over me. I went to the bathroom quickly and discovered my deepest fear: I was bleeding. My husband and I quietly dismissed ourselves without alerting the family and headed to the emergency room. An ultrasound confirmed what we already knew: Our baby had passed. The little life that had been growing inside of me wasn't meant for this world.

They scheduled a dilation and curettage (D&C) for the following day. I was scared as I'd never had surgery, and this surgery would be the period on the end of this pregnancy. They put me under, wheeled me to the operating room, and what felt like thirty seconds later, I awoke, sobbing, in the recovery room. It was over. My baby was gone, and I had failed again.

What happened next will stay with me as long as I live. In my darkest hour, my friends and family descended on me with love. If you are close to me, you know I love Tazo chai tea, and I was given a case of it. All of my favorite creature comforts surrounded our home: Oreos, flowers, Coke, trashy magazines, cozy blankets. I was even given intangible gifts like my girlfriend just sitting with me as I cried at our loss. That weekend was Maddie's second birthday party, and my nieces spent their vacation baking cakes and cake pops for our guests. These women surrounded me with love in such an incredible way. It would have been easier for them to send a card, but instead, they rolled up their sleeves and did the hard things. They loved me with an unconditional love, and it will forever be my favorite testimony of the hands and feet of Jesus when I wasn't even able to move.

We are made from love to love. Does that make sense? The Lord loves us with an everlasting love, and then, once He created us, our greatest commandment from Him was to go love people. Literally, the reason you are here is love. We are called to love one another with the love given to us. What does active love look like? It looks like baking cakes when there is a need. It looks like sending flowers when you are far away. It looks like your girlfriends, lying in bed with you as you sob and beg God for answers. This is the kind of love that the Bible speaks of over and over again. Romans 12:9 tells us to love genuinely. With all that you have and all that you are, love people freely. Give of yourself without hesitation in their dark times.

This is my command: Love one another the way I loved you. This is the very best way to love. Put your life on the line for your friends.
John 15:13 MSG

When you are in need, what would make you feel the most loved? Friends coming over with Kleenex and cookies? In your most trying times, how could your friends love you best?

How do you show love to your friends? Do you love them well?

LOVE YOUR FRIENDS

Jesus, make us loving friends. Make us the kind of friend that you are to us. Give us the capacity and willingness to love people in our lives deeply. Thank You for being the ultimate depiction of love by dying for us.

Lord, show us how to love our friends in the way that each of them needs to be loved. Help us to appreciate our friends and the seasons they are in.

Amen

DAY NINETEEN

Comparison

If you are like most Americans, the second your eyes pop open in the morning, you reach for your phone. And I can tell you that the easiest way to ruin your day is to jump on Instagram and peruse the lifestyles of the Instagram famous. Their houses are never dirty, they are always dressed in brand new clothes, they are always quaffed, and their children wouldn't dare throw a temper tantrum. Before you have even gotten out of bed, you are behind. Your morning breath could melt paint, your kids are already fighting, and the pile of laundry in your hallway seems to multiply every night.

I have a dear friend who is always put together. She clearly wakes up early each morning and spends a good amount of time putting herself together. When she arrives at school, her hair is curled, her makeup is done, her nails are never chipped, and she is gliding in on the cutest wedges. Now, I would never darken the doors at school because my newest drop-off attire consists of my ratty Walmart jammies and a fuzzy robe. If you think I am joking, please ask my mortified daughter.

Now, I could easily spend my life feeling badly about myself because I look like the creature from the Black Lagoon in the mornings, but I would really rather get an extra hour of sleep than do my hair. What is so great about our friendship is that neither of us cares how the other one looks. I can admire her beautiful composure, and she can admire...something that I do well. I am no better than she, and she is no better than I, but we both adore each other because of who we are to each other.

So many times, we get caught up in the comparison game that we become unable to function. This voyeurism into each of our lives has paralyzed us from living freely. God tells us in Galatians 6:4–5 to be who He made each of us to be. Don't try to be someone you're not because that is not who you are made to be. Use the gifts and talents God gave you to be the best version of yourself. And while you're at it, be genuinely happy for other women whose gifts and talents are different than yours.

James 4:1–3 says that we get nasty and mean when we compare ourselves. When we are out for our own gain, we turn into mean girls, and that is not who we are called to be. God created us uniquely on purpose. Your unique talents and gifts are yours to own and to use creative license with. When you operate in your gifts, you are contributing to the world in a way that only you can. We need you. Without you, we are incomplete. So, if you show up to school drop-off with a messy bun and yesterday's mascara, own it. If you wake up early and walk into that school with your fresh manicure and a beautiful new winter coat, girl, work it. At the heart of it, we're all the same: We want to be seen and loved. And guess what? We see you, and you are deeply loved just the way you are.

Make a careful exploration of who you are and the work you have been given, and then sink yourself into that. Don't be impressed with yourself. Don't compare yourself with others. Each of you must take responsibility for doing the creative best you can with your own life.
Galatians 6:4–5 MSG

Maybe Instagram doesn't trigger you to compare yourself to others, but something else does. List that thing here.

Now, I want you to pray and ask the Lord for two things: Ask Him for forgiveness for not loving yourself exactly how He made you and forgiveness for comparing yourself to others. Then, spend some time thanking Him for who you are, how you look, and your unique gifts and talents. He made you just right!

COMPARISON

God, thank You for making each of us so different. Thank You that there is only one of each of us out there. Lord, show us how to be more appreciative of the women You created us to be. Show us how to use our gifts to honor You and honor women. Forgive us when we have coveted what other women have and not appreciated what we have. Forgive us for believing we are inferior because our lives don't always look a certain way.

Now, God, we ask You to fill us with love and admiration for women in our lives. Help us to be women who build each other up and appreciate each woman just as You made her to be.

Amen

DAY TWENTY

Treat Yo' Self

For our entire marriage, my husband Josh has worked weekends at various churches. He is home during the week with our boys while I run my Young Living business. He is able to do some work during the day, but mostly, he's raising our boys. We are very blessed to be able to say that we are both home everyday with our kids.

Josh is the patient one in our marriage. He is also the patient parent. That is not my inherent gift. Because I work for myself, I am able to be home with our kids during the week, but then, I am full-time Mommy on the weekends. As our roles shifted a bit with our businesses, we were careful to make time for each of us to get away from wiping butts, making grilled cheese sandwiches, and breaking up fights. While children are a blessing and a gift, there is really only so much Paw Patrol you can watch before you are sure your brain is going to explode.

If either of us is starting to get that wild look in our eyes, we look at each other and say, "Go. Leave. Get some space." Now, for Josh, my precious, introverted husband, his times for himself are spent alone, enjoying a quiet lunch or watching a basketball game on his tablet. He is a man of simple pleasures. He is also rejuvenated and recharged when he is alone.

This is so not me. Remember how I said that my sister and I call each other and say, "I can't be alone with my thoughts right now"? I am the extrovert in our marriage. My tank is filled up when I am with good friends (and good food, if we're being real). If I am heading out to shop, I want a girlfriend or 12 with me. God made me to be a woman who craves that connection with her friends, and the amazing thing about it is that these times serve multiple purposes. Not only am I getting a breather from Mommy duties, but I am also being filled to the brim by women who build me up, pray for me, laugh with me, cry with me, and speak life into me. I am getting a little bit of Jesus when I take time for myself. I am a better wife and a better Mommy when I take time to get refreshed.

I know so many women who struggle with taking time for themselves for various reasons. I know that there are extenuating circumstances that make it difficult: no sitter, no money for a sitter, a special needs child, bedtime with our children. Believe me, some seasons of life make it nearly impossible to get these times away. I promise you though that if you make it a priority to get away, you will feel better in every aspect of your life. Even Jesus had to get away from the hustle and bustle to just be alone with His friends and to pray (Luke 5:16). It is so important for us to get away—it is even away! When your husband grumbles about you leaving the baby with him, whip out your Bible and show him this verse!

Girl, get away. If it's possible, get out once per week for just an hour to relax and refresh. If you can't swing that, then do what works best for your family. And get with your girlfriends who will build you up and do life with you. These are the times when you share your heart, your hopes and dreams, your struggles, and everything in between. These are the friends who will sharpen you (Proverbs 27:17) during each season of your life. I promise it's worth the juggling act to take time for yourself. Your family will see the difference in you, and you will be better for it.

And He said to them, "Come away by yourselves to a secluded place and rest a while." (For there were many people coming and going, and they did not even have time to eat.)
Mark 6:31 NASB

Do you make getting away and taking time for yourself a priority?

How can you schedule time for yourself each week or each month?

Think of a time when you were able to get away and refresh.

TREAT YO' SELF

Lord, thank You for our families. Thank You for our spouses and our children. Thank You, Jesus, for the gifts that they are in our lives.

Lord, reveal to each woman reading this how valuable her time away getting refreshed can be to her family. When it seems like it's too difficult to get away, God, make a way. Bring the right group of friends to each woman's life that will encourage her, lift her up, bear her burdens, and breathe life into her. Thank You for good friends who add value to our lives. We are truly blessed!

Amen

—DAY TWENTY-ONE—

Abide

When God put this study on my heart, I journaled that I didn't know what it would look like, only that I knew I was supposed to write. A few days later, I began making notes, and the word abide came up frequently. Then, I opened my Bible to 1 John, and every other word was abide. Loud and clear, Jesus. I spent the next couple of weeks studying the word to be sure it was the right fit. Abide's definition is to accept without objection. When I thought of friendship and abiding, I found that these two things go hand-in-hand.

What God has placed on my heart for each one of you is a spirit of community. I think, as women, we always feel like we are missing out and that other women have everything that we want. In the months leading up to me writing this, a myriad of messages flooded my inbox with women expressing that they, too, had the same longings and desires for friends. They shared their losses, their pain, their shame, and the light bulb went on: We all have the same draw toward friendship. You may be sitting there believing that you are alone, but please hear me: You are normal. The desire for deep, intimate, godly friendship is normal because it is how God made us. We are created for community and companionship.

My prayer for you is really amazing friendship with people just like you. I prayed for years for great friends, and my prayer wasn't answered immediately. Actually, it took years for the first good ones to enter the scene. I promise you that God is faithful, and there is a reason you are in a season of waiting. When the waiting is over though, girl. You're going to see how much He loves you.

And when you find your tribe, abide. Abide in Jesus, abide in love, abide in each other. Your heart will be full, and you will see just a glimpse of the vast love that Jesus has for you.

Abide in me, and I in you. As the branch cannot bear fruit by itself, unless it abides in the vine, neither can you, unless you abide in me.
John 15:4 NASB

Do you know how much Jesus loves you? If it were only you here, He would have died for just you. And that incredible Jesus abides in your heart. Take some time to let that wash over you.

Lord, thank You for the opportunity to write this love story to women all over. I ask that You would bring deep, meaningful friendships out of this study. I ask that You would fill the voids that so many of us women have in our hearts. Thank You for making us the way You did. Thank You for the desire for community so that we don't have to do this life alone.

More than anything, thank You for abiding in us so that we get You every single day. Teach us to abide more deeply in You and then, to love freely. We love you so.

Amen

Made in the USA
Las Vegas, NV
27 August 2021